D1106082

DATE DUE

M. Haley			

DEMCO 38-296

Rollin'

Monster Trucks

by James Koons

CAPSTONE PRESS
MANKATO

C A P S T O N E   P R E S S
818 North Willow Street • Mankato, MN 56001

Printed in the United States of America.

Library of Congress Cataloging-in Publication Data
Koons, James, 1970–
   Monster Trucks/James Koons.
   p. cm.
   Includes bibliographical references (p. 45-46) and index.
   Summary: Discusses the history of monster trucks, first built in 1974, as well as advances in their design and construction, and the races and events in which they appear.
   ISBN 1-56065-371-X
   1. Monster trucks--Juvenile literature. [1. Monster trucks. 2. Trucks. 3. Truck racing.] I. Title.
TL230.15.K66 1996
636.1'6--dc20

                                   95-43218
                                      CIP
                                      AC

Photo credits
Peter Ford: 4-20, 24-42
Dennis Pernu: 22
USHRA: cover

Table of Contents

Words in **boldface** type in the text are defined in the Glossary in the back of this book.

Chapter 1

Monster Trucks

Monster trucks are the biggest pickups in the world. No two monster trucks are the same. They are made by hand.

People give their monster trucks wild paint jobs. They want their trucks to look more exciting than other trucks.

Monster trucks are too big to be used on the road. They are driven in mud races and car-crushing contests.

There are almost 400 monster trucks in the world. People go to stadiums, arenas, and fairgrounds to see the trucks. You might have seen a monster truck on television.

No two monster trucks are the same.

Monster Truck Races

Monster trucks have loud engines. Some people in the stands wear earplugs when the trucks race. Most races last less than three seconds. In that short time a monster truck uses up to five gallons (19 liters) of fuel.

Workers stay up all night to make the mud pit where the trucks race. They mix truckloads of dirt with gallons of water. It is hard work.

When the monster trucks' huge tires spin, they throw mud into the stands. Some of the fans get sprayed. Even fans in the balcony might get splattered with mud.

Monster trucks are driven in mud races and car-crushing contests.

Chapter 2
Monster Truck History

A man named Bob Chandler bought a blue 4x4 pickup in 1974. A 4x4 is a pickup with **four-wheel drive**. The engine can turn all four wheels. This gives the pickup more power. It gives it better traction.

Chandler lived in Hazelwood, Missouri. Few people in Hazelwood owned a 4x4. Chandler had to fix his 4x4 himself when it broke down. He was good at fixing 4x4s.

Other 4x4 owners asked him to fix their trucks. He opened a repair shop. He parked his

There are 14 Bigfoot monster trucks.

own blue 4x4 in front of the shop. It brought in new customers.

The First Bigfoot

Chandler added parts to his 4x4. He added a huge set of tires. His truck attracted more and more people to his repair shop.

Chandler liked to race his truck. Because he drove it fast and hard, it broke down a lot. His

Monster truck bodies are made of fiberglass.

Some moviemakers have put Bigfoot monster trucks in their movies.

friends told him he pressed the gas pedal too hard when he raced. They called him Bigfoot.

Chandler liked the name, so he painted it on the side of his truck. Bigfoot was born. It was the first monster truck.

Bigfoot Travels

Bigfoot was more powerful than any other 4x4. No one wanted to race against it. Chandler knew it was a special truck. There was no other truck like it in the world.

He wanted other people to see it. He loaded it onto a trailer. He took it around the country. People paid money to see the monster truck.

Moviemakers paid for Bigfoot to be in their movies. Some toy makers made Bigfoot toys.

More Bigfoots

Chandler made money from his truck. So he made other Bigfoots. He hired engineers to design them. He hired mechanics to fix the trucks when they broke down.

Today, Chandler owns 14 Bigfoot trucks. Each one is blue. Chandler does not drive the trucks in competitions anymore. He hires drivers.

People pay money just to see the monster trucks.

Chapter 3
Making Monsters

Monster trucks are not made in factories. They are built piece by piece. Engineers design the trucks on computers. It takes a year to design a monster truck.

Mechanics build the trucks. They follow the engineer's instructions. They find the parts the engineer wants.

Sometimes they cannot find the parts. Then they make them or hire someone to make them. Sometimes the driver is also the engineer and the mechanic.

Drivers detail their trucks to make them look better.

Monster truck tires are terra tires. Terra tires are made for farm machinery.

The Engine

The engine gives a monster truck its power. Most monster trucks have engines from cars or other pickups. Mechanics use powerful engines from cars like Corvettes, Mustangs, and Cadillacs.

The engines have eight **cylinders**. A special fuel called methanol is forced into the cylinders. The methanol mixes with air. A

16

spark explodes the mixture. The explosions push
a piston. A piston is a can-shaped piece in each
cylinder. When the pistons move, they spin a long
rod. The rod is called a **drive shaft**. When the
drive shaft spins, it turns the wheels.

Modifying the Engine

Mechanics **modify** the engines to make them
more powerful. They **bore** the cylinders. This
makes the cylinders larger. Larger cylinders allow
larger explosions. Larger explosions push the
pistons and drive shaft even faster.

Mechanics add blowers. These force more fuel into the cylinders. More fuel makes larger explosions.

Some mechanics add another **carburetor**. A carburetor mixes the methanol and the air. **Dual carburetors** force more fuel into the cylinders. Larger cylinders and more fuel create larger explosions.

The Body and Chassis

Fans do not see a monster truck's engine. They see its body and how it is painted.

The first monster trucks had metal bodies. They were very heavy. They broke or were crushed if the trucks jumped or rolled over.

So engineers made **fiberglass** bodies. They are made from **molds** that look like the original metal bodies.

Fiberglass bodies are lighter than metal ones. They are easier to fix. If fiberglass gets cracked or dented, it can be patched and repainted.

Drivers paint their trucks and give them crazy names.

The truck body is attached to a frame called a **chassis**. It is made of metal tubing. The chassis is strong. It has to take the hard bumps without breaking.

Detailing

Drivers do many things to make their trucks look better. The things they do are called **detailing**. Detailing does not make the trucks run any faster. But drivers still like it because it makes the truck look better.

Monster truck drivers add chrome trim to their trucks. If a part is not painted, they want it to shine. Some use polished aluminum.

Drivers also paint their trucks wild colors. They give them crazy names. Some of the names are Bear Foot, Overkill, Snakebite, and Wildfoot.

Monster trucks do not have real lights. Instead, their lights are painted on the frame.

Drivers have sponsors to help them pay for their trucks. In return, the drivers paint the sponsors' name on their trucks.

They weigh less without real lights. Lighter trucks go faster.

The Cab

Some drivers have plain cabs. These have a seat, a steering wheel, and gauges. There is nothing else in the plain cab.

Other drivers like fancy cabs. They detail the cab to match the body. Many of these cabs have loud stereos.

Tires

Monster truck tires are terra tires. Most are five and one-half feet (nearly two meters) tall. Terra tires are made for farm machinery. They work great in the mud. They are perfect for monster trucks.

Some monster truck drivers shave their tires. Shaving takes rubber from the **tread**. It makes the trucks lighter and faster. Shaving can take off up to 200 pounds (90 kilograms) per tire.

Some drivers shave their tires to make the trucks lighter.

Axles and Suspension

Sometimes engineers design monster trucks using parts made for other vehicles. Many engineers use **axles** from school buses. Bus axles are stronger than regular truck axles.

The truck's suspension system connects the tires and axles to the chassis. Its job is to absorb the hard bumps. The suspension system makes the ride feel smoother.

The suspension system is made of springs and shocks. The shocks are filled with a special gas.

Four-Wheel Steering

Monster trucks are heavy. This makes them hard to steer. Some trucks have four-wheel steering. With four-wheel steering, the driver can turn both the rear wheels and the front wheels. This makes turning easier. Bob Chandler invented four-wheel steering.

Many truck makers use axles from school buses. Bus axles are stronger than regular truck axles.

Sponsors

Monster trucks are expensive. Many drivers save their money for years before they build one. Once the truck is built, it costs a lot to keep it running.

Drivers have sponsors to help them pay for the truck. Sponsors give the drivers money. In return, the drivers paint the name of the sponsors on the trucks.

Chapter 4

Monsters Compete

People liked Bigfoot. Some fans made their own monster trucks. The drivers got together to hold shows. Some drivers would see whose truck could pull the most weight. They got this idea from tractor pulls.

At other shows, the trucks were put on display. People liked the truck pulls and the displays. But they wanted to see what else monster trucks could do.

Car Crushes

Bob Chandler decided to crush some old cars with one of his Bigfoots. He lined up a

The first monster truck war was held in the Silverdome in 1984.

few junk cars in a field. He drove Bigfoot over the cars. A few of Chandler's friends were with him. One of them videotaped the crush.

Crushing at the Silverdome

Chandler brought his car-crushing stunt to a truck and tractor pull at the Silverdome in Pontiac, Michigan.

During a break in the show, he drove Bigfoot to the middle of the dome. Two junk cars were parked there. He revved his engine and crushed the cars.

None of the people had ever seen this stunt before. The crowd loved it. People ran onto the field to get a closer look at Bigfoot.

The car crush was the first competition invented just for monster trucks. Promoters bought old cars from junkyards. Many people came to see the monster trucks crush cars.

The First Truck War

The first monster truck war was held in the Silverdome in 1984. More than 70,000 people

Early monster trucks were not strong enough to take high leaps.

WLTE FM 103

paid to see it. Bigfoot was there. Some of the other trucks there were King Kong, Invader, Barefoot, and Taurus.

The trucks took turns crushing a row of junk cars. Unlike today's monster trucks, these trucks did not jump very high in the air. The monster trucks at the first shows were not strong enough to take high leaps.

Truck makers worked hard to make the trucks more exciting. They made them stronger. They made the engines bigger.

Promoters started using ramps. They put them in front of the junk cars. Monster trucks became the high-flying crushers we know today.

Mud Bogging

Fans got tired of watching monster trucks crush cars. Promoters came up with mud racing. Drivers and fans call it mud bogging.

Mud bogging drivers see who can drive the farthest through deep mud. The best way to get through the mud is to drive as fast as possible.

Strong springs and shocks absorb the hard bumps.

Drivers race two at a time. The winner of one race goes up against the winner of another race. The races continue until only two trucks are left. Those two trucks race to see who is the champion.

Obstacle Course

Another monster truck event is the obstacle course. Obstacle course drivers race around an oval track. They race two at a time.

On the track are hills, dirt ramps, tight corners, and piles of junk cars. The trucks fly high in the air. They twist and turn around barriers.

The first truck to cross the finish line is the winner. Oval track racing takes more skill than mud bogging.

Monster Truck Thunder Drags

The Monster Truck Thunder Drags are held once a year. They take place at the RCA Dome in Indianapolis, Indiana. The competition began in 1990.

The Monster Truck Thunder Drags are held once a year at the RCA Dome in Indianapolis.

The drivers compete in several events. They earn points for how well they finish in each event. The driver with the most points wins. The winner is the world champion.

Chapter 5
Safety and Rules

W hen more people started to make monster trucks, Bob Chandler worried about safety. Many drivers had little experience. They were likely to cause accidents. Some owners were putting huge engines in their trucks. These engines were too large for the truck bodies.

Chandler wanted to prevent accidents. He started a safety group called the Monster Truck Racing Association (MTRA). The MTRA set rules for safety. The rules will not let dangerous engines or drivers compete in shows.

The Monster Truck Racing Association sets rules for safety. Every truck is inspected before every race.

All trucks have a roll cage in case the truck rolls over.

Officials inspect every truck. They make sure the trucks are safe. All drivers go to a meeting before the race. There, the officials explain the rules.

Roll Cage and Harness

There is always the chance that a truck will roll over. So all trucks have a roll cage. The driver sits inside the roll cage. The driver will be protected if the truck rolls over.

A harness keeps the driver inside the roll cage. The harness is like a seat belt made for racing. It is stronger than a regular seat belt.

Other Safety Equipment

Every truck has a kill switch. It turns the engine off if the driver rolls over or loses control. Turning the engine off lowers the chance that a fire will start. The pit crew can flip the kill switch by remote control.

There is a fire extinguisher in every cab in case a truck does catch fire. The extinguisher is always within reach of the driver. It is one of the parts checked before each race.

Drivers wear clothes made of fire-resistant material.

Every truck has an engine shield between the driver and the engine. It separates the cab from the engine. It protects the driver in case the engine explodes or catches fire.

All drivers wear a helmet. They wear clothes made of special fire-resistant material. The material does not catch fire easily.

Emergency Crews

Safety crews work at every monster truck event. They are trained to deal with emergencies. Some of them are on the fire crew. They have fire extinguishers and a water truck. If a truck rolls and catches fire, the crew quickly puts it out.

At least two emergency medical technicians are also on hand. They are called EMTs. They are trained to take care of any injuries to the drivers.

Every truck has a kill switch. It turns the engine off if the driver rolls over or loses control.

Genuine
Copenhagen/SKOAL
Genuine
Draft
IT AIN'T EASY BEING GREEN!

Chapter 6
Other Monsters

When the first monster trucks were made all pickups were large. Since then, smaller pickups have become popular. They use less gas and are less expensive to run.

Some people are making monster trucks from these smaller pickups. They do not have as much power as the larger trucks. They compete only against other small trucks. It would not be fair if a big truck raced a small truck.

Smaller monster trucks have become popular. They use less gas and are less expensive to run.

A Car-Eating Mechanical Dinosaur

In 1990, a new monster appeared. The monster is called Robosaurus. Robosaurus is a giant robot that crushes cars. It looks like a dinosaur. It is made by a company called Monster Robots. They make robots for movies.

Robosaurus is more than 40 feet (12 meters) tall. Two drivers sit in its head. They control the claws and jaws.

Robosaurus can pick up a car and tear it apart in its jaws. Then the robot blows fire from its mouth.

Fans Around the World

Bob Chandler made his first Bigfoot more than 20 years ago. Monster trucks have come a long way since then.

Millions of people pay to see monster trucks every year. The sport that began in a small town in Missouri now has fans in countries all over the world.

Engineers design monster trucks with computers.

Glossary

axle—rod that connects the wheels

bore—to make a cylinder larger by grinding its walls

carburetor—device that mixes fuel and oxygen before they are forced into the cylinders

chassis—frame of a vehicle on which the body rests

cylinders—can-shaped areas of an engine that hold the pistons where gas is ignited

detailing—custom work done to the visible parts of a vehicle

drive shaft—long rod that connects the engine to the wheels

dual carburetors—two carburetors on one engine

fiberglass—plasticlike material made from glass fibers

four-wheel drive—special feature that allows the engine to turn all four wheels

modify—to change an engine to make it more powerful

mold—pattern used to shape something

tread—groove patterns on a tire that make it grip the ground better

To Learn More

Atkinson, E.J. *Monster Vehicles.* Mankato, Minn.: Capstone Press, 1991.

Bushey, Jerry. *Monster Trucks and Other Giant Machines on Wheels.* Minneapolis: Carolrhoda Books, 1985.

Holder, Bill and Harry Dunn. *Monster Wheels.* New York: Sterling Publishing, 1990.

Johnston, Scott D. *Monster Truck Racing.* Minneapolis: Capstone Press, 1994.

Johnston, Scott D. *The Original Monster Truck: Bigfoot*. Minneapolis: Capstone Press, 1994.

Sullivan, George. *Here Come the Monster Trucks*. New York: Cobblehill Books, 1989.

You can read articles about monster trucks in *Off Road* magazine.

Useful Addresses

Bear Foot Racing Team
3710 Highway 11
Pontoon Beach, IL 62040

Bigfoot 4x4
6311 North Lindbergh
Hazelwood, MO 63042

Carolina Crusher
P.O. Box 151
Wadesboro, NC 28170

Special Events (Promoter)
804 North Delaware
Indianapolis, IN 46204

SRO Motorsports (Promoter)
477 East Butterfield Road
Suite 400
Lombard, IL 60148

United Sport of America
(Promotes Canadian Events)
2310 West 75th Street
Prairie Village, KS 66208

Index